No Helmet

Humorous Short Stories
about
Embarrassing Moments
in
Sports

JOHN SOWER

Copyrights © 2024

All Rights Reserved.

Preface & Acknowledgement

No one likes being embarrassed, and most want to forget our embarrassing moments.

However, sometimes people enjoy hearing stories about embarrassing moments that others have had - if they are humorous.

This collection is primarily of true, humorous short stories from our family and friends.

These stories are sometimes told, with varying amounts of elaboration, at family gatherings, often to uproarious laughter.

Time mitigates most embarrassment, and most

people involved can enjoy the humor.

We acknowledge the role of others in these stories that have made them humorous. Names are changed to prevent further embarrassment.

Table of Contents

Chapter 1: Helmet Humiliation 1

Chapter 2: Messing with Mabel 7

Chapter 3: Seasick Social Scientist 12

Chapter 4: Embarrassed on Skis 19

Chapter 5: Beer and Biking 24

Chapter 6: Missing in Majorca 28

Chapter 7: Barnyard Diving 35

Chapter 8: Bluefish Bedlam 40

Chapter 9: Forgotten Ferns 48

Chapter 10: Not WrestleMania 53

Chapter 11: Futile Fishing 58

Chapter 12: Snare Drum 65

Chapter 13: Cheerleader 68

Chapter 14: Willie Nelson 71

Chapter 15: Red Right Return 74

Chapter 16: Hit it! 80

Chapter 17: At the Messiah 85

Chapter 18: In the Sistine Chapel 90

About the Author 93

Chapter 1: Helmet Humiliation

Friday night high school football was a tradition in the American Midwest in the 1950s. We lived in a small community, and everyone liked football. My father was a professor, and we had a 100-acre farm and had to feed beef cattle every night after school. Previously, we had no time for team sports. I was a freshman and was excited to be on the football team.

I was tall, so I became a defensive end. If a running play was toward me, my job was to get outside the ball carrier and turn him inside so the linebackers and linemen could tackle him.

It was a night game, and the lights were on. This was junior varsity, so we usually played on Thursday nights instead of Friday. Sometimes, if the varsity had a game out of town, we would play our game on Friday.

Being on a football team in front of the home crowd was exciting. Most high school students attended – even for the Junior Varsity games. Also, many adults attended either because they were parents or friends of the players or because there wasn't much else to do on a fall Friday evening in a small Midwest town. This was before large-screen TVs and the internet.

I was never much of an athlete, but I enjoyed being on the team with my friends. As a freshman with no experience, I was on second-team defense. I probably would have been on third-team defense if there were enough players to have one.

The coach was an American history teacher with a brusque manner who no one liked. I never had him as a teacher, but his style was reportedly only to sit and read aloud from the textbooks.

The first game was close, and the first-team defense played the whole game, so I didn't get into it. I don't remember what happened in the second game, but I didn't get into it either.

In the third game, our team was ahead by two touchdowns, so in the middle of the third quarter, after a time-out, the coach yelled, "Second-team defense." This was it! My first time in a football game! We excitedly jumped up and ran onto the field. I was exhilarated. It was exciting. I ran onto the field with my friends on the second-team defense.

My problem starts with the fact that I have an extra-large head and wear size eight hats. As an adult, I have one criterion when shopping for hats: Can I find one big enough? Our small school only had two size-eight football helmets for the junior varsity—one was maroon, and the other was white. This was a home game, so we were wearing white uniforms with white helmets.

The realization of my disaster hit me when I reached the middle of the field:

I HAD FORGOTTEN MY HELMET!

There I was, in the middle of a football field, with 11 players on the opposing team wearing helmets and ten on our team wearing helmets—and me standing there like an idiot without a helmet.

I was humiliated – embarrassed beyond measure. I panicked – how stupid could I be? All the students, parents, teachers, and neighbors in the bleachers were looking at me. I froze. What should I do? Was I going to be ridiculed for this for the rest of my life?

With thousands of high schools and perhaps

millions of high school students playing every Friday night, why was I the only one to forget his helmet in front of the home crowd?

My life passed before my eyes in a flash. I seemed to have three choices:

1. Play without a helmet. I vaguely remember some old photos of Ivy League football players with shoulder pads but no helmets. Was that possible? I discarded that quickly.

2. Borrow a helmet from one of the first-team defense players leaving the field because the second-team replaced them. I looked at them, then remembered that because of my big head, there were no helmets on the first-team defense large enough to fit me. I had to discard that alternative as well.

3. The third alternative was to keep running across the football field past the visiting team bench, past the visiting team bleachers, across an empty field, into the woods near the river, and disappear in mortification forever. Maybe I could live in the trees like a hermit or hitchhike to California and assume a new name? This alternative seemed emotionally safe in the short run but impractical in the long run.

So, I turned around, ran back to where I'd been sitting, grabbed my helmet from under the bench, put it on, and ran back onto the field, making it in time for the visiting team's next play.

As I reached under the bench for my helmet, I heard the coach say something that wasn't complimentary. It might have been "jerk" or even "a-hole." I don't remember. When I ran back on the field, I don't remember if people cheered or jeered, what happened during the rest of the game, or what happened for the rest of my freshman football season.

I was permanently traumatized and embarrassed by the humiliation of my forgotten helmet.

The following year, as a sophomore, I saw some redemption. I was promoted to first-team defensive end because the sophomores moved to the varsity, and I was a starter. In the first game, the visiting team tried a quarterback-end run in my direction. I brushed aside the blockers, grabbed the quarterback with a horse collar tackle (now against the rules), spun him around, and threw him down in front of the visitor team bench. That was very satisfying.

In the second game, their large fullback began an end run my way. I vaguely knew him because he was a friend's cousin at our school. Again, I got outside the blockers, dove at him low, got his knees together, and brought him down hard. He said, "Nice tackle," as he got up and returned to his huddle. Again, it was very satisfying.

My high school football career ended in the third game because my knee was bent sideways, and I had to have surgery for a torn cartilage. The surgeon said no more football.

So, while my forgotten helmet humiliation was my most embarrassing moment ever, I enjoyed my time on the football team and regretted not being able to continue to play.

Chapter 2: Messing with Mabel

In the early 1950s, we had a 100-acre farm in Michigan. My father was a professor, but he was raised on a farm and thought the experience would benefit his sons. Also, he didn't like the stock market and preferred buying land as an investment. We had beef cattle, pigs, and chickens, and we grew corn, wheat, alfalfa, oats, and barley to feed the cattle.

When we were out of the country for a year during my seventh grade, my father had others farm the land, which continued after we returned. The barn and outbuildings sat empty and unused. My brother and I did not miss having chores like feeding the cattle every day after school or being embarrassed by showing up for school with smelly cow manure on our shoes.

One day, to our surprise, a chicken appeared in the barn. We don't know if she lived there for the year we were away or whether she wandered from another farm and decided to stay. Also, to our surprise, she laid an egg – perhaps her gesture of payment instead of rent. We put a round bar of soap on the spot where we found the egg. She considered it her nest and continued to lay eggs, but I don't think we ever ate them. During the day, she would wander the grounds searching for food; we named her Mabel.

Rural people in the 1950s had a more casual attitude about guns than urban dwellers today. I was 13 and my brother was 15. He had a 22 rifle and a single-barrel 16 gauge shotgun. I had a pellet gun, which was like a 22 rifle. Later, I bought an Ithaca double-barrel, 12 gauge, claw-hammer shotgun from a neighbor for only $2. We casually kept the shotgun in the kitchen closet with the brooms and mops. The shotgun shells were on the shelf, along with the work gloves and hats. As I said, rural people were casual about guns.

Our tranquil life with Mabel ended abruptly one evening when, after supper, we heard her cackling and shrieking hysterically. Something horrible was happening.

We rushed out of the house only to see an animal, maybe a fox or raccoon, running away in the darkness and Mabel clucking and cawing inside the barn. She looked horrible. Her head was bloodied, and it looked like one eye was missing. Whatever it was had eaten half of her head.

She calmed down after a while, and although still bloodied, it seemed that she would live.

We were furious. How could an intruder invade our property and do so much damage to Mabel? We never had any animal attacks in the years when we'd been farming and had cattle, pigs, and chickens in the barn.

We felt we had to do something! Mabel had to be avenged! We had to get him!

The next night, we put Mabel in a crate with a large stone on top in our side yard – right outside the 2nd-floor window of the bedroom my brother and I shared.

We opened the window to hear Mabel, put the crate under the yard light, and went to our bedroom with our shotguns ready.

Where were our parents as we retreated to our armed aerie? In the bedroom next to ours and not very concerned.

We watched the crate from the window and tried

to stay awake. However, we drifted off and woke up startled when we heard Mabel cackling and shrieking in panic. We grabbed our shotguns and tried to stick them out the window. We hadn't realized that the window screen would be a problem as it hung from hooks at the top, and as we pushed the screen away and stuck our shotguns out the window, the screen swung back to us, pushing the barrels of our shotguns down so we couldn't fire them from the window.

Frustrated, I grabbed my loaded Ithaca 12 gauge, double-barrel, claw-hammer shotgun and ran from our bedroom, down the hall, down the stairs, through the living room, through the dining room, across the kitchen eating area, and through the screened-in porch. At that point, I cocked the claw hammers, leveled the shotgun, and fired both barrels in the general direction of Mabel's crate.

A double-barrel 12 gauge shotgun has enormous recoil force, and I found myself kicked back onto the porch steps. A full-grown, strong man would have trouble staying upright after firing both barrels together. I don't remember where my brother was or whether he had come downstairs and fired his single-barrel 16 gauge shotgun at the intruder. Maybe he had more sense.

I didn't see the intruder, and I no longer heard

Mabel. At first, I feared I had killed her with my tumultuous double-barreled blast.

After picking myself up, I froze in horror. My father's brand new lime-green Plymouth sedan was in the dark, on the other side of Mabel's crate. What had I done? Had I hit it?

I don't remember anything else. The intruder didn't get Mabel, who lived with us for years, albeit with a strange half-eaten head. My father's car wasn't damaged. The intruder never came back. If nothing else, my shotgun blast scared him off.

I was horrified and embarrassed at what I'd done. I never fired my shotgun again, and a year or two later, I loaned it to a friend who never returned it.

Tranquility returned to our small Midwest farm, but it took me a long time to endure the embarrassment of wildly firing my double-barrel, claw-hammer, Ithaca shotgun.

Chapter 3: Seasick Social Scientist

Seasickness can be very serious. My father took the Queen Mary to Europe at the start of World War II. It went alone without protection from German submarines going north to the Arctic Circle, going very fast (over 30 knots/hour) and zigzagging constantly to avoid torpedoes.

Its purpose was to carry troops to Europe, and they retrofitted the cabins and put four stepladder bunks where there previously was a single bed. Each sleeping space was claustrophobic, with only a foot and a half height between bunks. The 10,000 soldiers had to sleep in shifts and wait on deck or the lounges when not in the bunks on their rotation.

My father was seasick immediately and spent

most of the trip huddled in blankets on the deck, even though it was winter, because he was nauseous when cooped up in his cabin. He could eat very little, and he was cold, sick, and miserable. The week-long trip was a nightmare for him.

When we were young, my parents built a summer cottage on a lake near Petoskey in Northern Michigan. My father loved fishing, and we had favorite places on the lake for family fishing excursions to catch sunfish and bluegills. However, his favorite fishing activity was rowing his boat slowly and peacefully across the lake in the evening with a single fishing pole with a lure called a flatfish in search of walleye pike.

Happiness for him was arriving home with a big walleye pike on a stringer, which my mother would prepare for our next day's supper.

When I was 13, we lived in Ceylon (now Sri Lanka) for a year. My father flew ahead to find housing, schools, and a car. En route home, he flew ahead of us to Germany to purchase a car so we could spend several months touring Europe.

He joined the family for the last leg of our trip – on the ocean liner returning home from England. This is when we learned how desperate his seasickness was. He was ill as soon as we felt the movement of the waves after leaving port. He spent most of the trip on deck as he couldn't go to the cabin or the dining room without feeling nauseous.

When we sat down for a meal, he would come in, grab a few dry rolls, and retreat quickly to the open deck. There were long rows of chaise lounges for passengers facing the sea. He turned his chair the other way to stare at the wall, as the up and down motion of the ship while watching the ocean made him sick. We always knew which chair was his, and ungraciously, we teased him.

Years later, while building the summer cottage in Michigan, he met some construction workers, many of whom were from a nearby Indian community. They, too, liked fishing, and as construction progressed, so did the fish stories.

They all decided to go fishing together, but not on our small lake. Instead, they would venture into Little Traverse Bay, a part of Lake Michigan, and instead of walleye pike, they would go fishing for lake trout – which can get very large. This was a new type of fishing for my father, and he was excited.

They met at the public dock and went out in a boat owned by the Indians. Little Traverse Bay is deeper, nearly 150 feet, than our small lake, where the depth was 40-50 feet, so fishing strategies differed. The Indians loaned my Dad a rod and reel more suited for the deeper water.

It was a windy day, and the waves came from the west across Lake Michigan. There were whitecaps on the waves, scenic from the shore but rough going in a small boat.

Why the name Little Traverse Bay? The French traders would travel in large canoes around the Great Lakes in search of furs to ship to Europe. They would come down from the tip of Northern Michigan and "traverse" (cross) the Bay as they headed South. Hence, it was called Little Traverse Bay compared to the Grand Traverse Bay, which is further south and takes longer to cross. Traders in canoes could reach the Mississippi and Missouri Rivers by going to the SE Corner of Lake Michigan, carrying their canoes from one river to another, and continuing what some consider the first cross-country route in America.

To reach the lake trout at lower depths, they used heavy steel fishing lines. This was my father's first experience with steel line. The trouble with steel lines is that if one isn't careful, the line will back up on the reel and jam.

Due to the waves, it was tough for my father to hold the fishing pole with one hand, hold his thumb over the steel line on the reel to prevent it from jamming, and hold onto the side of the boat, which was plunging up and down with the heavy waves.

His line got jammed, and he needed two hands to

straighten it. As he looked down, concentrating on the fish line, he felt a surge of seasickness coming. Meanwhile, the two Indians had their lines out and were excitedly talking about their prospects for fish. They could see that my Dad was having problems but were a little insecure and shy about helping him fix it. They knew he was a professor at a large university and were a little intimidated.

Then it hit him. He knew he had no choice. He was going to be sick. He calmly reached into his mouth, removed his false teeth, looked over the edge of the boat – and vomited. Afterward, he put his false teeth back into his mouth and continued to try to fix his fishing pole.

The two construction workers had never seen anything like that before – and were speechless. No word was spoken on the boat for several minutes. Finally, my Dad looked at them, smiled, and threw up his hands in despair about the jammed reel. They smiled back, and all had a good laugh. They each made several imitative gestures of pulling out their teeth, vomiting over the edge, and then putting their teeth back in their mouths.

History didn't record whether they resumed fishing (I think not) or caught any lake trout on that trip (I know not). The weather was getting worse, and my father wasn't getting better, so the Indians reeled in their lines, and they all headed home.

On reaching the dock, they found a welcoming party of two Indian wives, three aunts, and five children ages 4-6. They had been waiting at a playground high above the Bay and could see the returning boat.

The wives and aunts were anxious to see the distinguished professor who had gone fishing with their men. As they were being introduced, one of the men spoke rapidly in Indian dialect with the gesture of reaching for one's teeth, vomiting, and then putting back. More words were quickly spoken with more gestures, and soon, everyone, including the children, was laughing, gesturing, and smiling at my Dad.

On reaching solid ground, he immediately felt better, so he smiled and, although embarrassed, joined in the laughter. He even took his teeth out once more in front of everyone and showed them. The children shrieked in delight and asked him to do it again – but once was enough.

Everyone said goodbye and went their separate ways. During the next week, the workers told their friends working in nearby cottages, so soon all my parents' neighbors knew the story and repeated it, using gestures and all, to others.

My Dad was a good sport but was embarrassed for a long time.

He never went lake trout fishing again in Little Traverse Bay.

Chapter 4: Embarrassed on Skis

When I was in my 20s, I thought Boston would be the perfect place to live because it was home to young people, universities, great beaches at Cape Cod, and good skiing in nearby Vermont and New Hampshire. The beaches and the ski slopes were both within an hour or two.

I had skied in New England, Colorado, and Michigan (our home state), often with my other brother, who was a better skier than I was. I preferred the intermediate slopes, typically marked by blue squares. Black diamond slopes were too difficult, and double black diamond slopes, especially with moguls (bumps), were to be avoided.

Mount Sunapee's website lists 67 trails on 230

acres with a top elevation of 2,743 ft. The slopes had approximately four times the vertical drop of the ski resorts back in Michigan.

The technology of skiing has changed dramatically. In the 1960s, we had 6-foot-long Head 360 skis with cable bindings, which are old-fashioned and unwieldy by today's standards. Skis now are higher tech, shorter, and wider on the front and back, permitting skiers to better "carve" in the snow when turning. Sadly, I retired from skiing before these skis were available.

Large ski resorts like Mount Sunapee in New Hampshire have easy, gradually declining slopes for beginners, wide, medium slopes for intermediate skiers, and steep slopes for experts.

The ski slopes are maintained regularly by enormous caterpillar vehicles that "groom" the trails. On a typical ski trip, skiing on different slopes just for the variety is fun.

My brother and I were skiing Sunapee with his girlfriend, Cheryl. He had more girlfriends than I did. Cheryl and I were intermediate skiers, but my brother was an expert.

Sunapee had a long winding trail on the far left side (when going downhill) called Ridge Trail. I presume it's still there. It was very narrow, and under normal conditions, it would be considered an intermediate trail.

New Hampshire had experienced a week of cold weather, with temperatures dropping to zero degrees every night, making the ski slopes icy. It had not snowed recently, so there was no fresh snow on the trails. Ridge Trail wasn't flat like most intermediate trails; it was bowl-shaped, with both sides sloping upward.

Skiers control their speed by zigzagging (tacking in nautical terms) down the slope and using the edges of their skies to dig in and reduce their speed – at least, that is the theory.

The zigzagging is easy on wide slopes with soft, fresh snow. It's an entirely different matter on a narrow, bowl-shaped slope where the snow is frozen like glare ice.

When a group is skiing together, the least skillful skiers usually go down each section of the slope first so that if they get in trouble, the more experienced skiers who follow can help them.

In our case, Cheryl ventured down the slope first, made it safely, and stopped several hundred yards downhill to rest and wait for us. As the better skier and her date, my brother followed and stopped 25 yards uphill from her.

No Helmet

This was the last day of our ski trip, and I was tired. This ski trail was like an icy chute, and I found it impossible to zigzag or control my speed.

Approximately 30 yards uphill from my brother, I lost control and fell, and because of the icy steep slope, I couldn't stop sliding. To prevent broken legs, getting one's skis sideways on the slope downhill from one's body is best to try to slow down and control one's speed. On an icy, steep, narrow chute, getting on one's back may be best to prevent a leg from being caught underneath, resulting in a leg injury.

This is where the disaster started: I couldn't stop sliding. It was too icy. It was like an icy slide at a playground. I slid down the hill on my back, slowly picking up speed. I got closer to my brother and tried to stop – but couldn't. Instead, I plowed into him, knocked him over, and together, we rolled over and over while sliding down the icy chute.

We couldn't control our skis, which intermittently got caught in the ice or with each other, so we were rolling over and over, head over heels, skis and ski poles everywhere, picking up speed, and headed toward Cheryl—like a giant rolling human snowball.

Cheryl's eyes got huge, and she panicked and tried to climb up the edge of the ski slope out of our way. However, together, my brother and I slid into her, knocked her out from under her, and she fell on top of us.

The three of us rolled over and over and slid another 50 yards down the steep, icy chute before we could get control and stop.

This was embarrassing, infuriating, and hilarious. I was afraid I'd ruined my brother's relationship with Cheryl forever. She seemed upset, embarrassed, humiliated, and angry.

I was humiliated—one of my most embarrassing moments ever. My brother was upset with me, but staying angry about such a hilarious incident is impossible. No one was physically hurt, but our pride and my brother's romance were severely damaged.

I went skiing many more times, but only on the less icy slopes of Colorado or closer to home in Maryland.

Cheryl disappeared from my brother's life, and I never heard anything about her again.

Chapter 5: Beer and Biking

We were four Americans in our 20s—two men and two women. On the surface, we looked like two couples traveling together. We had just met and were waiting for visas to attend an international work camp in Nigeria. We had spent a week in a suburb of Paris and decided to take the train to visit Amsterdam.

After checking in at a Pensione, we spent the day in the art galleries and ended up at the Heineken brewery. We took the tour and enjoyed the free beers and food in the Heineken beer garden. It was a pleasant afternoon.

We were a little intoxicated, and in a burst of enthusiasm, I suggested we rent bikes and ride out into the Dutch countryside – so we did. The bike ride was beautiful as we rode past the canals, windmills, and scenic Dutch landscapes, which reminded us of the art we'd seen at the galleries.

We rode our bikes about 10 miles from Amsterdam, fueled partly by the Heineken beer and hearty Dutch food. The bike riding seemed so effortless, like maybe we were in better condition than we'd realized.

After a while, it became cloudy, and we decided to head back to the Pensione.

Then it hit us: We had been enjoying a strong tailwind, and in our Heineken-induced state, we hadn't noticed. We turned around to head back just as the sky got darker and the wind picked up—except that now it wasn't a tailwind; it was a headwind.

The ride back was grueling. We had to put our heads down, grit our teeth, and ride against the wind. A cold, sobering headwind replaced the Heineken-induced euphoria we had experienced riding out of town.

It got colder and windier, and none of us were appropriately dressed. One of the girls had sandals, which were fine for strolling around art galleries but not for hard pedaling into the wind. The other male,

Jacques from California, had only shorts and a light shirt, and despite the hard pedaling, he began to shiver in the cold.

We stopped to rest several times when we could find shelter from the wind, but we were afraid of getting stuck out of town on our rented bikes and getting lost in the dark.

One girl disparagingly commented that this was my idea and asked why I hadn't considered the wind and the distance before we left.

I was upset and embarrassed.

We were hungry, thirsty, and very tired, but there was nowhere to stop for water, rest, or refreshments. What had been scenic canals and windmills on the way out now became nightmarish images in the dark of a poorly planned excursion.

We finally returned to the Pensione and collapsed in our beds, exhausted. They did forgive me the next day as they realized we had all participated in the decision to go for the bike ride, and no one had thought about the time of day, a change in the weather, the potential headwind, or the rigorous ride home.

We had all gotten "over-served" at the Heineken Brewery.

We made it back to Paris and then to Rome on a

slow overnight train from Parks that stopped in every town along the Italian coast, got our vias, flew to Nigeria, and participated in the International work camp.

It was the experience of a lifetime, but I'll never forget the embarrassment of our return bike ride after visiting the Heineken Brewery in Amsterdam.

Chapter 6: Missing in Majorca

Majorca is a Spanish island in the Mediterranean. We visited my wife's friend Billy, who had a house near a small village on the West side of the Island – away from the development and tourist activities. Our sons were 10 and 13.

Billy was a semi-retired livestock broker. He was the man to call if you needed a few exotic cattle to balance or enhance your herd anywhere in the world. He had an open house with wide porches and gardens only a few minutes from the village. His house overlooked a valley and had a pleasant afternoon breeze.

We walked to town every morning for fresh bread and fruit and to chat with the shopkeepers and neighbors. We watched the bocce games in the town square in the evenings and listened to music from musicians in a small bandshell. We understood why Billy chose this idyllic village in Majorca to retire from his life of global travels and cattle-dealing.

Majorca was influenced by many cultures throughout history, including Phoenicians, Romans, Christian Byzantines, and Muslim Arabs before the Spanish. Majorca is a popular tourist destination for visitors from Northern Europe, especially in the winter.

En route, I traveled with my younger son to Majorca and had a four-hour layover in London. I considered waiting at the airport but decided to show him some of London instead. We took the train to Waterloo Station, briefly toured Westminster Abbey and saw Big Ben, double-decker buses, the Thames, changing the guard at Buckingham Palace, bobbies in uniform, and left-side drivers before returning to Heathrow Airport by taxi. Not many people can say they saw London in four hours, but I don't know how much my son appreciated or remembered the short visit.

On the first day in Majorca, we went on a tour. Because I was familiar with Mediterranean beach culture, I spotted several topless girls at the beach, but I didn't think my sons noticed.

The next day, my wife said Billy was taking her shopping for her art and antique store. I had been looking at the hiking trails and saw an inverted "U" shaped trail where we would hike to the top of a mountain, walk along a ridge to our right, and return to town on another trail. I was an experienced hiker and assumed I could follow the trail map.

We packed some water, fruit, and bread and headed out. The first trail was easy. Signs said it was an ancient Christian pilgrimage route. In my imagination, I saw long lines of the faithful with donkeys carrying supplies on their journeys. It was a flat, well-worn trail, and we saw mountain goats cavorting high above on the cliffs. Looking at them from far below stirred my acrophobia (fear of heights).

Based on my experience with similar-sized ski slopes, I estimated we hiked a couple of miles and were about 1,500 feet high. We started looking for the ridge trail to our right, but no trail markers existed. We needed the Appalachian Trail Club, with its slash marks on trees.

We turned right off the pilgrimage trail and hiked on what I thought was the ridge trail for about a quarter of a mile. There were no markers, but the ground was open and easy to traverse. I kept looking to our right on the map for the trail that would return us to the village.

The terrain below looked rougher than the easy pilgrims' trail we were on before. I couldn't find anything resembling another trail.

I could see the port town far on my right—my lodestar—so I knew we could keep going in the right direction.

I considered returning along the ridge and taking the pilgrimage trail home – probably a wiser decision in retrospect, but I kept expecting to find the missing trail.

When we left, the weather was sunny, but we didn't have a forecast. This was before cell phones, so we were on our own. It became cloudy, and the wind picked up from the north. For the first time, I was concerned.

Finally, I decided we had to bushwack and hope we'd find the trail or an accessible route. For non-hikers, Webster defines bushwacking as "to travel by foot through uncleared terrain."

The boys were in fine shape and having a good time, so I wasn't worried about them. I didn't expect to see wolves or mountain lions.

We descended the mountain around rocks, trees, thorn bushes, and loose dirt. It was fun initially – a rugged adventure, and the boys enjoyed it. We soon had scratches on our arms from the thorn bushes, but we kept going.

We finally found what appeared to be a trail and started following it. It was very steep and rough going. Downhill would appear easier than uphill as it's less taxing on the lungs, but there is more risk of falling.

We entered the beginnings of a canyon, but I slipped while scooting over a large rock, fell awkwardly, and twisted my knee. The boys were initially amused to see me fall but soon realized I was in pain and would have trouble walking. We decided to stop and rest and finish the snacks and water we had with us.

I found an old tree branch I could use as a walking stick, knocked the branches off, and started hobbling down the mountain.

I hadn't noticed that the sky had darkened more or that the wind had picked up because we were in a canyon. Now, I started to worry.

We kept going slowly down the mountain but soon realized that the canyon was a trap that was turning and taking us in the wrong direction – almost directly away from the town.

I considered climbing out of the canyon and searching again for the mystery trail. Then, I decided that if we kept going downhill, we would emerge in civilization somewhere.

My knee was sore, and I had to stop and rest again. The boys were patient and still enjoying themselves.

I assumed that Billy and my wife were back from shopping and wondered where we were.

We were tired because bushwacking is difficult after a full day of hiking. Every step required concentration to avoid loose rocks or thorns – or both.

It was nearly dark, and we had a long way to go. The wind was starting to howl. We had come over halfway down the mountain and still saw no trails.

Finally, as it got dark, we stumbled onto an overgrown cart trail. Perhaps farmers had used it to tend their olive orchards. I assumed it must lead someplace, so we took the route away from the town and headed downhill.

After a half hour in the twilight, we reached a road and could turn toward town.

We finally made it home, but Billy told us he was just about to call the home guard, report us missing, and start a search party. My wife was upset and worried. We learned later that the trail map was a local joke.

We were all tired, and I was sore and humiliated. The boys had a good excursion, and a long, hot visit to Billy's outdoor jacuzzi was welcome.

It took a long time to stop feeling embarrassed.

Chapter 7: Barnyard Diving

I've been horseback riding only three times. Each was a worse disaster than the one before. We were raised with farm animals like steers, pigs, and chickens, but we never had horses. My father was a professor, and his interest in the farm was for long-term land investment and short-term character-building for his two sons (The jury's still out on that).

I don't remember much about my first horseback riding trip except that I was about ten. I got up on a platform to get on the horse. It seemed to sag in the middle, so I got up his rump. Any equestrian knows that's wrong, and as I soon learned, horses don't like it. He bucked me off fast, and when I fell, my pride was hurt, and I didn't try again for years. Mid-west professors don't buy into the cowboy culture of having their sons get back up there and try again.

The second time was 20 years later when my brother and I stupidly combined horseback riding with a few vodka and tonics and, after bouncing around for an hour or so, discovered raw sores on our backsides. We were embarrassed that our wives had to apply salve and bandages. We knew nothing about horseback riding and didn't know how to keep our weight on our feet to prevent butt-side friction burns.

In the mid-1980s, my mother suggested the whole family (four adult children, three spouses, and five grandchildren) go to a dude ranch in Colorado for a week. Her friend said it was a wonderful family bonding experience, so we agreed.

The most fun for me was taking our two sons, ages 10 and 13, to the country western store to get fitted out for the dude ranch. They excitedly ran around getting cowboy boots, hats, shirts, neckties, scarves—the whole works.

The dude ranch was in a beautiful mountain valley setting. There were cabins for each family and a common dining room. It was in the mountains in central Colorado, close to the Colorado River and downstream from the "Never Summer" Mountains.

The first morning's drill was for the wrangler to assess our riding skills and assign a horse to us.

We joked that they matched the horses to our personalities. Steamboat, my horse, was large, calm, and easy-going compared to my wife's horse, Rixey, who was prickly, high-tempered, and kicked at anyone behind her.

It had rained the previous week, and the ground was still muddy. Inside the corral, the ground was a sodden mess of horse manure and mud.

The first exercise, to demonstrate that we were sufficiently skilled to take horses out on the trails, was that we each had to ride our horse in a trot in a square in the corral. This meant three right turns and a complete stop.

Everyone in the family completed the drill before I did. I was the last to go. My wife was an experienced rider who sat comfortably in the saddle and knew what she was doing. The boys often visited their grandparents in Boulder, CO, who used to take them horseback riding. They smoothly rode their horses through the drill.

Everyone waited anxiously because they knew I was nervous and didn't know how to ride. Were they secretly hoping I would fall into the mud-manure?

Steamboat and I started our trotting routine, but

no one had ever told me to keep my weight on my feet, not my bottom, so I bounced uncomfortably. We made the first and second right turns satisfactorily, but then Steamboat decided to go left back to the barn on the third turn. The wrangler, anticipating this, shouted, "Turn him right," which I later learned meant showing the horse who was boss.

So, I made him turn right, and suddenly, he started to gallop. Again, not knowing how to ride, I bounced uncomfortably. Then, the drama began.

After sprinting the last leg of the square, Steamboat stopped very abruptly. It was more than abrupt; it was like I had lassoed a steer in cowboy movies, and Steamboat's job was to pull him back. It was like a 1,000-lb horse hiding behind a solid glass wall, or as I concluded later, it was Steamboat's way of getting revenge on me for making him turn right.

When he stopped, the momentum kept me going, and I fell forward on the back of his neck. The upper part of my body was horizontal – precariously hanging parallel to the mud-manure. My body teetered forward, and my head fell to the level of Steamboat's right eye, and I concluded what his intent was as he seemed to be saying, "Gotcha, Succa." (translated: "Got you, sucker")

Out of the corner of my eye, I could see the combination of horror and glee on my sons' faces as

I started diving down over the horse toward the goo. I couldn't see, but I knew my older brother had his fingers crossed, hoping for a dramatic splashdown.

At that second, I was desperate. I was about to dive headfirst into the mud-manure in front of my young sons, brothers, parents, wives, and children.

Would this be my defining moment? Would the phrase "Barnyard Diving" be the epitaph on my gravestone? Is what they would remember about me for generations?

I think "pulling leather" means grabbing the saddle horn, but I was way beyond the saddle horn—it was now behind me. Desperately, I held on to Steamboat's neck and managed not to fall off. Slowly, I slid back, regained my composure, smiled at my family, walked the horse to a dry area, and dismounted. I had saved myself and my pride, as I hadn't dived into the goo.

I thought I saw a sly smile on the wrangler's face as he took Steamboat's reins – like it was a standard joke to try to dump the rider.

So, I was very embarrassed, but I somehow avoided "Barnyard Diving" that day, and I introduced a new phrase into our family lore.

Chapter 8: Bluefish Bedlam

Great Point is at the end of a five-mile barrier beach peninsula on the Northeast corner of the Island of Nantucket in Massachusetts. It's our favorite place for surfcasting for bluefish.

Bluefish are rapacious fish that swarm up the East Coast in the Spring and return in the fall. They appear in large schools, devouring the bait fish in shallow water along the shore. They are aggressive fighters that are fun to catch, although their meat is oily and not a favorite on seafood restaurant menus.

We had to wake up at 4:30 am to make it to Great Point by dawn – the best time to catch hungry bluefish. My brother Dave was visiting, and we were well equipped with 12 ft surfcasting rods, Penn reels with 20 lb line, Hopkins triple hook lures, and sand spikes to hold the fishing rods so the sand wouldn't get in the gear mechanism. I also had long-necked pliers for removing hooks, which I carried on my belt.

On other trips, I took my filet knife with a 10" blade for cleaning fish on the beach in a knife holster on my belt like James Coburn, the knife thrower in the Magnificent Seven movie.

Ominous dark clouds surrounded us as we drove in the four-wheel-drive jeep from the small town of Wauwinet along the beach to Great Point.

Our timing was perfect. The first rays of dawn peeked out of the clouds as we parked; already a half dozen four-wheelers and 8-10 men leisurely surfcasting from both sides of the Peninsula. Typically, the locals let the guests practice their casting first – a polite way of having them test the waters until the great schools of ravenous bluefish come crashing through the shallow water near the shore. When the locals see a few bent rods, they know the fish have arrived, so they set down their coffee (or beers in the evening), exit their comfortable four-wheelers, grab their fishing rods, set up sand spikes, and join the fray.

During the hot summer, the bluefish are small, 3-4 lbs., and easy to pull in. In the spring and fall, however, larger bluefish (10-12 lbs.) arrive and are more of a challenge.

The clouds suddenly covered the nascent sunrise, and the sky darkened. The wind picked up and whipped salt spray on us. The waves, from across the Atlantic, crashed at our feet. Most men were barefoot in shorts, and some had windbreakers. Seagulls drifted with the wind above us, looking for edible morels, and we saw a few terns that fishermen knew indicated the bluefish schools were near.

We joined the surfcasters 8-10 feet apart, starting at the end of the peninsula. Dave was on my left, and we were facing East. There was a lazy rhythm of occasional surfcasting – to keep testing for the arrival of the morning's prey.

We could see occasional lights on the far horizon – from boats out toward the famous, or infamous, Georges Bank sandbars where ships ran aground for centuries. Just imagine the terror of being in a storm in the middle of the night and drifting toward the sandbars – with only primitive navigation technology.

We could see the current moving north along the beach, but no bluefish.

Were we going to be skunked this morning? Had

we gotten up early and endured a problematic hourlong drive on the beach for nothing? Were we to tell our wives that it was a beautiful and exhilarating sunrise – but no fish? Doesn't one hate to use that line? But hope springs eternal.

Suddenly – wham! Two fishermen had simultaneous strikes, and their poles were bent over as they struggled with their fish. We could tell these were not small fish. One guy was caught off guard, trying to hold his coffee in one hand and fight his fish with the other. He tried to set his coffee down, but the coffee spilled out, and the paper container caught in the current heading North from our right to our left. It may cross the Nantucket Sound and reach the shore at Hyannis on Cape Cod near the Kennedy compound.

Two more guys had strikes, and there were two more bent poles – and then I had one, and a few seconds later, Dave had one. Mine had struck in shallow water so that I could pull it in quickly. It wasn't large – and I used my fishing pliers to remove the hooks and let it go.

Years later, on the same beach, I stood next to my 8-year-old son, who hooked a large bluefish and was stalemated, trying to pull it in. After watching him struggle, I suggested he use his legs instead of his arms, and he pulled in the fish by walking backward halfway across Great Point.

Today was bedlam. It was exciting. It was crazy. Men were yelling and groaning as they struggled to pull in their fish; waves were crashing, gulls were screaming, terms were diving frantically, and fish were flopping in the wet sand. We could taste the salt from the spray whipping off the waves into our faces.

Dave had hooked a large one and was having trouble with it. The fish was far out, and he feared losing it. This must be a school of monster bluefish that were very hungry.

The atmosphere changed. The wind was blowing harder, and the terns were dive-bombing, looking for food scraps from smaller fish that the bluefish were attacking. Some guys were shouting at each other; others were groaning as they tried to pull in their large fish. One could see them adjusting the drag on their reels to reduce the pressure and the risk of breaking the line and losing the fish. Two guys got their lines entangled and were yelling at each other.

Then disaster struck; Dave's fish bolted to our left—with the current—straight toward the other fisherman. Dave had to reel in rapidly to keep pressure on the line and move to his left to keep up with the fish without entangling the others. He got past the first guy by lowering his head (and rod—

while keeping his rod tip up) and getting under the arc of the guy's bent rod and line.

His fish kept moving to our left, and Dave couldn't set his footing and pull him in. The drag on his reel released more line, allowing the fish to get further away.

He bumped into the next guy, who protested but who had his fish nearly in so he could duck under Dave's arc of bent pole and line.

It got worse; the fish had made it nearly around the corner of the end of the Peninsula, and there were five guys between Dave and his fish.

The first guy was a gentleman. He pulled in his line and waved Dave through.

The second was older, had a giant fish, and was straining to pull it in. Dave tried to get under the arc of his rod and line, but the guy wasn't strong enough to hold his rod up, and it smacked Dave on the back as he went under. I don't think he meant to – he was just out of control.

There are only three more guys to get past.

Disaster again! Dave tripped and fell on his knees and one hand. Miraculously, he held the rod and reel out of the sand, kept his hand on the reel, and kept the rod tip up while I ran over and pulled him up.

The third guy was a jerk. As Dave approached, he tried to wave Dave off. I was concerned because he had a long, slender filet knife hanging from his belt. Could this be trouble? When Dave lowered his head to go under the arc, the guy kicked at him, lost his balance, and went down on one knee in the water—just after Dave made it through on his hands and knees.

The fourth must have been the jerk's buddy because he tried to hold his rod with his left hand, reel in his fish with his right hand, and bump Dave with his hip to keep him away. Dave dodged him and somehow got past.

There was one more guy. As Dave started under the arc, the guy yelled as the fish tossed the lure. Under the pressure of the bent pole, the triple-hook lure soared back toward both of their faces—but thankfully, it missed.

Finally, Dave was alone with his fish. By now, he had rounded the corner on his left, facing North. He was exhausted and mortified by the embarrassment of his ordeal, but left alone, almost anticlimactic, he could reel his fish in.

The fish was enormous—one of the largest I'd seen, well over 12 lbs. I released the hooks, took a picture, and let him go. Dave looked back at the line of fishermen, feeling humiliated and worrying he would never revisit Great Point.

By then, the run was over. All was quiet. Even the wind abated. The bluefish had moved on.

When Dave is stressed, he forgets to breathe, and his face gets flushed. By this time, it was crimson red. Still embarrassed but gracious, he went back down the line and apologized to everyone. The rush had abated, so the guys were more relaxed. They all laughed, slapped Dave and each other on the shoulders, congratulated each other on their fish, laughed at the foibles of fishing, and returned to their vehicles to go home for breakfast. The guy with the knife cleaned his fish, put the filets in a bag, threw the carcass in the ocean, got in his car, and drove away.

Dave still felt embarrassed, but it had been an exciting bluefish run.

Chapter 9: Forgotten Ferns

Warning: Contains bathroom humor appreciated only by teenage boys.

Our family reunion weekend in Northern Michigan didn't turn out how we had hoped.

There were 17 of us from three generations: an 85ish grandfather, three married couples, a sister, and five grandchildren, including three teenage boys. I made the arrangements and found a small inn in Harbor Springs we could have for ourselves. It would be the first season for a young couple who were the managers and who had just graduated from culinary school and would be preparing our meals. It sounded terrific.

We arrived on a Friday evening, and the inn looked perfect. There were rooms for all of us, a beautiful dining area, and a large porch for my wheelchair-bound father. My brother and I had a tee time with our sons at a nearby golf course on Saturday morning while the others planned shopping and sightseeing trips in the historic, scenic small town.

The dinner the young couple prepared on Friday evening was inexplicable. It was a kind of fish stew, which they later explained had exotic and unusual ingredients. In retrospect, I should have explained that we were not gourmet eaters and that we preferred regular American food. I later wondered how fresh the fish was. They say you don't order seafood in the hinterland.

On Saturday morning, my brother's wife explained that he had stomach problems during the night and went to the hospital emergency room but had called and would return for our tee time.

I was busy organizing everyone's plans for the day, but we made it to the golf course on time. My brother joined us and said he wasn't feeling well, but I was distracted by checking in, helping the boys get organized, and hurrying to make it to the first tee on time.

We played the first couple of holes, but my

brother didn't do well and commented about his stomach. Again, I didn't pay much attention as I was focused on hurrying our sons along because they kept losing golf balls in the fern bushes along the fairways.

After teeing off on the fourth hole, my brother grabbed his stomach, said he would catch up with me, and rushed in an awkward, hunched-over manner toward a large patch of fern bushes. I wasn't sure if he lost a golf ball, wanted some fern boughs for his wife, or something else.

Encyclopedia Britannica says ferns are ancient – over 300 million years old. They are said to be very hardy, but I wonder if they are hardy enough to withstand my brother's visit. He said later that people having breakfast in the backyard of an expensive fairway-side home stared at him in horror as he stood up, emerged from the ferns, and adjusted his belt after he had relieved himself.

I began to understand my brother's embarrassment and severe health problems as the day progressed. Teenage boys may laugh, but diarrhea can be debilitating, and something he ate upset his stomach.

After a few more holes, he stopped playing and quietly rode along in the golf cart while we finished our round. He didn't eat much dinner on Saturday evening as he was still uncomfortable – or maybe because he didn't trust the chefs. Sadly, as embarrassed and uncomfortable as he was, he didn't know that the worst embarrassment lay ahead.

On Sunday, after I arm-twisted our host chefs into preparing a simple scrambled eggs breakfast rather than the avant-garde, edgy, experimental dishes they had in mind. Afterward, we packed up in four different cars and headed home. I have since wondered how fresh the eggs were.

My brother was in a car with three teenage boys – the worst type of group for people suffering from his condition. Soon after departing, he felt the pressure building up and became very uncomfortable. He feared he might have to stop along the highway and find more fern plants – or something similar.

After several hours on the highway, the pressure became insufferable, but fortunately, they had reached a state-owned rest stop with a restroom.

They all needed a break, so they headed for the bathrooms – my brother leading the way in obvious discomfort.

He ran the last 50 feet, bolted into the bathroom, and found a private stall. The boys followed into the room. After a few seconds, there was a large explosive sound from the stall, which stunned everyone using the facilities.

After an awkward silence, one of the boys, known for his sharp wit, quipped, "Could we have a courtesy flush, please?" The other boys howled with laughter and continued laughing for the 100 miles home, adding to my brother's embarrassment. Such is the nature of teenage boys.

Teenage boys have their own, sometimes disgusting, form of humor.

My brother was mortified with embarrassment.

How could that happen before his son, nephews, and family?

He recovered physically, but he suffered from sly smirks or comments from the boys for years.

Chapter 10: Not WrestleMania

It just wasn't fair. No one told him. No one expected it. He didn't know what to do. He was caught off-guard. If he had been warned, he would have done better.

What do you do if you're at the batter's box waiting for a pitch, and they throw a football?

Or if you're waiting to take a test, and the test questions they give you are in a foreign language?

In other words, some things happen for which there is no prior preparation.

As a freshman, he was small for his age. His mother said their family were late growers. He had hope because his older brother was over 6' tall in his senior year of high school, so maybe he would be, too. Now, as an adult, he's 6'5" and weighs 230 pounds, but in his freshman year, he was one of the smallest boys in his school.

High school wrestling is organized by weight. There are 12-14 weight classes ranging from under 120 to over 250 lbs. – approximately 10 lbs. apart. I remember guys in high school jogging with heavy clothes on while in the furnace room to get their weight down. Why wrestle in the 155 lb. class if you can get your weight below 155 lbs.?

Sometimes, there are huge guys over 300 pounds, but they get beat by a 250-pound wrestler if they are not quick, strong, and in shape.

Wrestling matches are held in gyms on large mats with referees. In team wrestling, the lightest class wrestlers start first, and the matches move up the weight scale, with the heaviest wrestlers going last.

Points can be scored for take-downs, escapes, and pinning. Also, points are awarded to opponents for lack of aggressiveness. Matches start from a neutral position with opponents facing each other and from a referee's position, where one wrestler is on his knees, and the other is on top on one side.

He was the lightest wrestler on the team, so his

match was first. Although he had never wrestled or seen a wrestling match, the referee waved him to the mat.

Then the referee waved his opponent to the mat – and IT WAS A GIRL!

He froze. He didn't know what to do. He knew a few girls, but he's never touched one except holding hands in a game at recess or church camp. He hadn't even been to dance class yet.

He had been raised to be a gentleman, and he knew girls' bodies were different than boys' and where not to touch them.

The referee brought them to the center of the ring, had them shake hands, and told them to start.

He stood there immobile. She was about his size and appeared to be scrappy. She recognized his indecision and dove for his legs. He kept them straight, avoided being taken down, and ended up on top of her – but she escaped and got a point.

What a disaster. The match had just started, and she was ahead. The referee started them in the referee's position with her on top, and he got away – so he got a point for an escape.

She charged again. He kept her underneath him but was afraid to reach around to turn her for fear of touching her breasts.

He later learned she came from a large family with many brothers and was accustomed to scrapping with them.

She charged again, and he held her off, but the referee gave her a point because he wasn't being aggressive.

The referee started them again, and she reached between his legs to try to turn him over – and she succeeded because he froze when her hand was grabbing near his groin.

She escaped again and got another point for his lack of aggressiveness.

The match ended. She had won. The referee held up her hand, and he snuck back to his side and hid behind his teammates.

They didn't tease him because they knew he was embarrassed. They, too, were shocked that a girl wrestled on the opponent's team.

Coed wrestling is more common now – but it wasn't then.

He was embarrassed, but the word didn't spread, and his friends at school either didn't know or didn't want to tease him. He didn't tell his parents for a long time.

He didn't stay on the wrestling team. Wrestling

with one girl was enough.

Sometimes, life hits you with the unexpected.

Chapter 11: Futile Fishing

She said she wanted to go fishing. She was a pretty 17-year-old, completing her senior year in high school, and preparing to move out and go to college. I was surprised she asked about fishing, but we believe in exposing her to as many different experiences as possible—even fishing.

I had fishing experience as a teenager during summers at my parents' cottage in Northern Michigan. Our cottage was on a three-mile-long lake with bluegills, sunfish, yellow perch, occasional smallmouth bass, and my Dad's favorite, walleye pike. There were a few other species, like catfish, and once, I caught a three-foot-long gar pike, an ancient fish with an elongated jaw and needle-like snout. My brother and I had fishing poles, boxes, and accessories, and I used to haunt the fishing supply stores in town when my mother went grocery shopping.

My most enjoyable fishing was surfcasting for bluefish in Nantucket in my 40s. Great schools would come crashing along the shore in the early morning and late evening to the delight of fishermen with 12' surfcasting rods.

Finding a place to fish near Bethesda, MD, was challenging. Unlike my home State of Michigan, which has 10,000 lakes, Maryland has only one, three hours away. The Potomac River is full of fish, but I didn't want to take her along the riverbank for fear she would slip and fall in and be pulled away by the current.

I explored charter fishing boats on the upper Potomac River (upriver from Washington, DC) but couldn't find one that would take three people. I wanted to take my granddaughter, my 40-ish son, who enjoys fishing, and me. Most charters wanted to take larger groups or just one person.

There is a fish drama in the River. It is known for largemouth bass, but in recent years, snakeheads, an invasive species, have spread. Both are aggressive predators, and one can imagine the subsurface warfare between them. Snakeheads are good to eat, but the name is a deterrent, so they are changing the name to one that sounds tastier for marketing reasons.

I visited Fletcher's boathouse on the Potomac River in Washington, DC, but my timing was poor. I was there the day they were closing the boat launch for the winter season. I noticed several boys fishing in the C&O Canal, which ran alongside the River, and wondered whether it was an option. I asked if there were fish in the canal, and they said yes.

The C&O Canal starts in Georgetown in Washington, DC, and runs 185 miles to Cumberland, MD. It opened in 1831 and operated for 100 years, carrying coal, lumber, and grain in mule-pulled barges. It was saved in 1954 when Supreme Court Justice William O. Douglas led an 8-day hike along the canal towpath and called for preserving it.

The canal bank was grassy, ample parking was available, and runners and kayakers were present, so it felt safer than an isolated site along the riverbank.

There was a small snack shop with fishing suppliers, and I was told there were both bluegills and catfish in the canal. There were sites with shade from overhanging trees where there were fish. And, by the way, one needed a fishing license in Washington, DC.

It seemed improbable that a DC fish and game warden would visit us, but to set a good example, I went online and got fishing licenses for my granddaughter, my son, and myself.

I had an 8-foot spinning rod and reel, and I purchased two small fishing poles with reels at the snack shop. I inquired about fishing strategy and was told that worms were the best bait, that one could get catfish in the shade if the bait were on the bottom, and the bluegills could be caught using a bobber that held the bait a few inches above the bottom of the Canal.

The next challenge was worms. I dug a few test holes in my backyard and checked under the flagstones in a walkway, but with no success. I returned to the snack shop and was told a local hardware store might have them. I checked with the hardware, and the young man went in the back and emerged with a box with nightcrawlers (large earthworms), but they were all dead.

It was late fall, and I had to give up on earthworms. However, I remembered taking my two young sons fishing on the dock in Nantucket and catching snappers (baby bluefish), scup (a panfish like bluegills), and sometimes a bizarre fish called a sea robin that had a hard square-fronted head, wings, six feet and barked when caught. Yes, that is true—look it up!

We would go to the fish store, purchase squid, rinse off the black ink, and slice the squid for bait – which worked very well. I wondered if the fish in the canal would like squid or shrimp instead of earthworms. I couldn't find squid at the supermarket or the fish store, so I bought fresh shrimp. Do you know how expensive fresh shrimp is?

I had kept my granddaughter and my son apprised of my planning, and we picked a warm Saturday morning and set up on the canal's bank. She was excited to go fishing.

I carefully cut the shrimp into little pieces, put it on a hook, put some sinkers near the hook, rigged up a small red and white bobber, flipped the ensemble into the canal, and instructed my granddaughter how to reel in the fish, and sat down to wait.

After a minute, I put several pieces of shrimp on a larger hook, put a weight on the line, flipped it toward the middle of the canal under the shade of an over-hanging tree, and sat down in one of my newly purchased folding chairs to wait for a catfish to take my bait and run.

Then, my 40-ish hedge-fund son showed up with my 5-year-old grandson. He brought his flyrod and amused himself by whipping flies out to the middle of the canal.

So, we waited. My granddaughter was enthusiastic and cheerful. And we waited. Nothing was happening, so we pulled in her line to discover something had eaten all the shrimp—without the bobber even quivering. These must be very clever and stealthy fish.

I rebaited her hook with more of that expensive shrimp, checked the bait on the catfish line, chatted with my grandson, who was amusing himself with some of his toys – and waited – and waited – and waited – and waited – and waited – and waited.

I rechecked her line and discovered the hook was bare again. I shifted to a smaller fishhook, hoping to catch at least a minnow or two – something to let her catch a fish. I checked my catfish line, and it was bare.

We weren't fishing; we were feeding expensive shrimp to tiny minnows. When we pulled in her line, she thought she saw a couple of micro minnows, but I didn't.

It reminded me of when I had an aquarium of tropical fish, and I saw pictures of tiny fancy guppies in their home environment of tepid ponds in third-world countries.

Sometimes, when surfcasting for bluefish at Nantucket but not catching any, we could comment on the beautiful sunset making the trip worthwhile as a feeble fallback for not catching fish.

Today, we had no fallback.

After a while, we called it quits. I had gone to a lot of work and built up her enthusiasm, and I was embarrassed. I thought I knew something about fishing but had utterly struck out. She was in good cheer and seemed to have enjoyed her outing.

My last comment was that I had promised to take her fishing, which I had done. Sadly, I couldn't guarantee we would catch any fish.

I am still embarrassed.

Chapter 12: Snare Drum

Sankaty is a magnificent private golf club on the island of Nantucket, MA. It is high on the bluff above the Atlantic Ocean, with beautiful fairways, especially with autumn colors in the fall. The afternoon winds and the gorse (shrub bushes) along the fairways can be formidable.

The process of becoming a member was rigorous. I had to list six members who knew me and indicate whether they knew me very well, moderately, or only slightly. I called one multi-auto dealer owner, a real gentleman I had met several times, and asked if I could say I knew him slightly. He laughed and said most guys don't bother to ask, and I could say I knew him well.

After five years of waiting, I had to have each of the original six references write letters saying they still recommended me. It was worth the wait.

I had limited playing privileges during my wait. On a windy afternoon, I was playing with my brother. On the 9th green, near the clubhouse, my ball was 110 yards away. I was hitting uphill into the wind, which requires a 9-iron for me. Sadly, I didn't look at my club closely, and I hit with the 6-iron instead. A 6-iron goes much further than a 9-iron.

The shot was a line drive that flew over the green and smacked into the side of the clubhouse. I was mortified to have hit the clubhouse but thankful I had not broken a window, but the noise was incredible – somewhere between a loud snare drum and a gunshot.

Several of the golf pros heard the noise and came running over. They must have thought it was a gunshot. As I mentioned, it was an uphill golf shot, so fortunately, I was on a lower level, and they couldn't see me.

I was dreading that they would drop me from the membership waiting list.

I deliberately did not rush forward and identify myself, and after a minute, the pros saw there was no damage, lost interest, and walked away. They saw my brother but didn't know him, so they didn't follow up.

I was very embarrassed, but I escaped recrimination and eventually was invited to join the club. I was a member for ten years and then, after a divorce, decided my days in Nantucket were over, so I dropped my membership.

It's a beautiful golf club, and I wish I could play it again.

Chapter 13: Cheerleader

She was blonde, perky, pretty, trim, and personable—a perfect cheerleader. The first football game was approaching, and she had an important role. High school football was important in the Midwest, and as the new cheerleader captain, she must do everything right.

The school tradition was that the pep band would play, the school cannon would fire, and the cheerleaders would lead the football team onto the field with their cute uniforms, pom-poms, and infectious enthusiasm.

They would run down the ramp onto the football field, turning cartwheels. The football players followed behind them and had been coached not to run them over.

It all started perfectly. The band played, the gun

sounded, the crowd cheered, and they were off. There were five of them, and they had practiced endlessly and could all turn perfect cartwheels. They were proud of themselves. She was the captain, the prettiest, the perkiest, and loved by all. And she was best at cartwheeling.

Something happened to her as the five cheerleaders ran down the grass ramp onto the football field. Just as she put her head down to turn her first cartwheel, her mind went blank, and she forgot how to do it. Rather than turning her body 90 degrees, putting her hands down, keeping her arms straight, and letting her momentum turn her, she collapsed. For a microsecond, she forgot how to turn a cartwheel. It was horrible; she fell like a rock and lay motionless on the field, stunned.

The four other cheerleaders performed their perfect cartwheels and ran down the field toward the home crowd. The football team, coaches, team helpers, and others rushed onto the field behind the team—except for the middle cheerleader, who lay crumbled in the grass, frozen in embarrassment. They split around her like a river going around a rock.

The football players ran onto the field, so attention was diverted onto them. The other cheerleaders ran to the home team bench and did

No Helmet

not notice her absence.

She lay there, humiliated, until several kind ladies walked over to help her. She wanted to dig a hole in the ground, cover herself with pom-poms, and stay there forever. She was in tears, sobbing in embarrassment, saying she could never be a cheerleader again. She walked off the field and sobbed for a long time.

Finally, she went over to join the other cheerleaders, pulled herself together, and performed her cheerleading duties for the second half of the game. At the next game, her cartwheeling skills resumed, and she was fine.

Sometimes tragedy strikes unexpectedly, leaving one humiliated and embarrassed.

Chapter 14: Willie Nelson

We had tickets to see Willie Nelson in an auditorium in the suburbs. It was a cold night, but I looked forward to hearing Willie. It was our second date; she was the third woman I'd known since suddenly becoming single the year before. I didn't enjoy the first date much, but I liked Willie Nelson and didn't want to go alone.

She wasn't ready on time, which wasn't a good start to our evening. We had a 30-minute drive to the auditorium, and we were late. There was no parking garage, but we drove around, found a space, and rushed to the auditorium in time to miss Willie's opening number. The concert was a disappointment because Willie had lost his fabulous musicality, and it sounded like he was merely reciting the well-known words in his songs.

We tried to get a drink at the intermission, but there was a long line and slow service. The lights started blinking before we could order, so we gave up and returned to our seats.

This date had not been going very well thus far. She seemed disquieted and bored, and I later learned she didn't like Willie Nelson—even when he could still sing.

We walked toward my car when the concert ended, but it wasn't where I thought it was. Other vehicles were leaving, and we still walked around looking for the mine.

I saw an adjacent lot around the building, and we walked to it and searched, but there was still no car. I wondered if it had been stolen. She complained about being cold and walking in heels.

The temperature had dropped; she wasn't dressed for it and was cold and unhappy. I walked her back to the entrance and told her I'd find the car and come pick her up. I returned to the parking lot and found a third area behind the building, and there was my car—finally.

I drove around to the front, but she wasn't there. I parked the car and went in to find her. She was seated in a warm waiting room, upset and feeling put upon. I was embarrassed that it took me so long to find my car, but when we arrived, I was more focused on finding a parking spot and rushing to the auditorium than remembering where I left it.

The drive home was cold and quiet. She commented negatively on my not remembering where I had left my car. Finally, we reached her house. I walked her to the door, said good night, and left. During our first date, she had hinted about my staying over some time, but tonight was not the night.

In retrospect, the evening didn't start well and got gradually worse. I was embarrassed about not being able to find my car, but I wasn't happy with her condescending and negative attitude.

It was an easy decision not to call her ever again. Sometimes, one cuts one's losses and leaves.

Chapter 15: Red Right Return

Experienced boaters understand the critical role of the thousands of red and green buoys that line rivers, port entrances, channels, and waterways. These markers are not just decorations but guides that keep boaters in navigable waterways. The 'red right return' rule, a fundamental navigation principle, dictates that boaters must keep the red markers on their right when returning to port. This rule is not just a suggestion; it's necessary to ensure they stay in deep enough water. Conversely, one keeps the red buoys on the left when leaving port.

Ignoring this rule can lead to severe consequences. For instance, if you casually ignore the red markers on your right when returning to port, you risk colliding with rocks, sand, and mud—or worse, running aground in shallow water. This isn't a minor inconvenience for shallow-draft pleasure boats, like waterski boats with outboard motors, but as I learned, to my embarrassment, it is a harsh reality for sailboats with heavy keels.

The unique island has 200 homes, a golf course, a boat harbor and marina, tennis courts, a pool, an elegant new clubhouse with several restaurants, and magnificent water views. It is small (2 x 3 miles), privately owned, and has a 24-hour manned gatehouse at the entrance. Only property owners, club members, guests, and delivery or repair services may pass the gate and get onto the island.

I enjoyed many rounds of golf, poolside lunches, club dances, tennis, and post-golf drinks in Adirondack chairs on the lawn overlooking the water.

The club newsletter said they had an Ensign day-sailor available for club members. The Ensign could be described as a recreational keelboat, which means it is heavier and more stable than sailboats with retractable centerboards, that are better for shallow water.

I was honest with the harbor master and explained that I had sailed on a lake at camp in the Midwest years ago. I thought I understood the basics and could handle the 22-foot Ensign, which had a mainsail and a jib sail (small sale in the front of the boat). However, I later realized that my understanding of sailing was incomplete, especially regarding the 'red right return' rule.

The first time out, I had help. My son had years of sailing experience and was on a team racing International One Design sailboats that only experienced sailors can handle. Years before, I had paid for him to join a group that raced former America's Cup sailboats. He easily managed the Ensign, and we sailed through the channel and out into the bay behind the Island. We were short of time, so we turned around and returned to the harbor.

The second time out, I had a friend, also an accomplished sailor, who had sailed over 20 Mackinaw Island races on the Great Lakes—from Chicago to Mackinaw Island and from Port Huron near Detroit to Mackinaw Island. He too easily mastered the Ensign, and we had a nice sail, although we were becalmed and delayed getting back to port.

Sadly, neither my son nor my friend talked much about what they were doing as they sailed the Ensign, or I didn't listen to what they said; thus, I didn't learn as much as I should have. In both cases, we had just finished playing golf and talked more about golf than sailing.

Finally, it was time to try it on my own. The harbor launch took me out to the Ensign, which was anchored in the back row of the harbor. I prepared the sails, unhooked the tie to the buoy, and launched. There was a moderate wind, ideally coming from a right angle to the channel. It was sunny and warm – perfect sailing weather. I was psyched! I sailed back and forth several times, practicing tacking (zig-zagging to go against the wind) and "coming about" (moving the mainsail boom when tacking).

Then, I made a big mistake!

I headed for the channel leading to the bay behind the island. Previously, we had entered the channel directly from the harbor. Today, I started from the back of the harbor. The red buoy was ahead of me on the left side of the channel, which meant it was on the right side when returning to the harbor.

I headed diagonally to the channel. I didn't realize I was in shallow water, and the Ensign's deep keel plowed into the mud. I should have returned to the center of the harbor and turned left, keeping the red buoy on my left. The boat was heavy (3,000 lbs), the keel was deep, and the mud was soft and dense. I was trapped, and the boat wouldn't move.

I lowered the jib sail and tried to turn the boat

with the main sail to escape the mud but was unsuccessful. I put the mainsail at half-mast to keep the boat steady. I tried to start the outboard motor, but it wasn't working, so that didn't help. So I just sat there stuck in the mud.

I had three choices:

1. Wait and hope another boat would come by and tow me.
2. Wait and hope the tide would raise the boat and I would get out of the mud.
3. Swallow my pride, admit defeat, and call the harbor master for help.

I telephoned the harbor master, who said he could see where I was and understood my problem, but he couldn't rescue me for at least an hour when the high tide would raise the boat.

So I sat there in the mud. Maybe it was my imagination, but half of the Island boating community chose that hour to pass by. Experienced boaters could instantly see my problem and what I had done. Most of them gave me a friendly wave while probably saying "Idiot" under their breath. A few just ignored me.

I was embarrassed. I was thankful I had been honest with the harbor master and not overstated my sailing prowess, but there was no excuse. I hadn't known about the 'red right return' rule as there were no channels on the lake where I learned to sail.

Finally, the harbor master came in the launch, hooked a line to the front of the Ensign, and towed me out of the mud. I lowered the mainsail, and he towed me to the Ensign's buoy. He said nothing, but I knew what he must have been thinking.

I was embarrassed and never asked to take the Ensign sailing again.

Chapter 16: Hit it!

Water skiing was very popular in Michigan in the 1950s and 1960s. The state has 10,000 lakes, and my parents had a summer home on one of them, Pickerel Lake, near Petoskey. My father bought a boat motor, and we waterskied frequently as teenagers.

We wondered why there were no pickerel pike in Pickeral Lake. There were northern, walleyed, and gar pike, but no pickerel pike. I did not see a pickerel pike until years later when I learned they were in the ponds on Nantucket Island in Massachusetts.

We had regular skis, short turnaround skis, and a slalom ski. We learned to jump the wake, start and finish from shallow water, and create pyramids (one guy on the shoulders of two others). We skied all over the 3-mile-long lake and through the channel to an adjacent lake.

Two decades later, my brother and I were married and planned a family reunion with our parents at Pickerel Lake. We decided to take our wives for a boat ride and show off our water skiing skills. My brother was driving the boat and suggested that I go first.

There was a procedure we followed when water skiing. One brother would drive the boat, and the other would be in the water with water skis on and holding a handle attached to a 75-foot ski rope fastened to the boat. The boat's driver would move it slowly in the water, enabling the skier to get in a good position to ski. The skier would crouch in the water, with knees bent, and when ready, yell "hit it" to the driver, who would gun the boat, pulling the skier out of the water up on his skis. The trick is for the skier to keep one's arms straight and knees bent until they are up on top of the water – and then stand up.

This starting procedure is hard to learn, and most beginners stand up too soon and then fall. My brother and I had repeated his procedure dozens of times.

We preferred skiing on a slalom ski, which was more maneuverable and fun. There were two ways to get started with a slalom ski: The first was to start with a slalom and a regular ski, get up on the water, circle around to the front of the house, drop off the regular ski, and proceed with only the slalom ski.

The second was to start from shallow water (5-6" deep) near the shore by standing on one foot in the water with the other foot in the slalom ski just on the surface of the water, getting the boat and tow line in position, pulling on the towline to create about 15-20 feet of slack, telling the driver to "hit it," and as the slack was taken up, stepping forward on the slalom ski.

A more advanced version was to start from the floating swim raft anchored in front of the summer houses. This is more difficult because one stands on the raft's edge on one foot, with the other foot in the slalom ski about 6" above the water, while waves rock the raft.

The strategy is the same: Line up the boat, pull it back to get slack in the line, tell the driver to "hit it," wait until the slack is taken up, and then step forward onto the slalom ski. We had done this many times, and it was the goal on this day because the water was chilly. If done correctly, one could ski back to the raft or shallow water and never get wet in the cold water.

My brother, both wives and our sister were in the boat. I was standing on the raft with the ski rope handle in my left hand, my left foot on the raft, and my right foot in the slalom ski hanging over the raft's edge. The wind had picked up, and the waves were rocking the raft.

My brother lined up the boat so it would go straight. I got the ski rope taught and pulled the boat back to create some slack. My brother, two wives, and our sister were watching intently.

Then, as I'd done maybe a hundred times before, I yelled, "Hit it!" My brother pushed the throttle hard, and the boat leaped forward.

Here's when I made my mistake.

I hadn't waterskied for over a decade, and it's not unreasonable that I might forget a key step.

Instead of waiting a few seconds for the slack to be taken up, I stepped off into the water immediately after saying, "Hit it."

The result was inevitable. I couldn't walk on water like Jesus, and I sank. Instead of skimming skillfully across the water on my slalom ski, I was disappearing under the water's surface. Then the slack tightened, and the ski handle jerked me forward.

At that point, I realized I had three choices:

1. I could hang onto the ski handle and try a new sport of subsurface water skiing,

2. I could try to get the slalom ski under me and rise out of the water.

3. I could let go and try again.

I risked having my arms ripped off, so I threw the handle in the air and sank into the water.

The spectators in the boat were shocked. Based on our overly confident talk, they had expected to see some skillful water skiing. Instead, they saw a splash, they saw me disappear under the water, and they saw the ski rope and handle fly up in the air.

There was no applause and no cheering. My wife, in particular, was unimpressed.

My brother was beside himself with laughter. He always enjoyed humorous human mishaps, especially when at my expense.

After everyone stopped laughing, we tried again and were successful, but it was anti-climatic compared to the spectacular and embarrassing start.

I was embarrassed; that was the last time I went water skiing.

Chapter 17: At the Messiah

The Messiah by George Frideric Handel is sacred and beautiful holiday-season music. It quotes Old Testament prophet Isaiah's predictions of the coming of the Lord. The performance was in a small auditorium and included a soprano from our circle of friends in the chorus, an orchestra, and four soloists: a tenor, soprano, alto, and baritone. My favorite parts are the tenor solos at the beginning and the trumpet towards the end.

We sat toward the front in the fifth row. An overweight senior citizen couple sat between me and the aisle on my left. My girlfriend (a funny word in one's late 60s) sat on my right next to our friend's husband.

No Helmet

As we settled into our seats, the announcer's voice echoed through the auditorium, reminding us to silence our cell phones, which we dutifully did. The air was thick with anticipation, and the venue's acoustics amplified a sense of expectation. The silence was so profound that even the slightest noise from the audience would have been disruptive. It was a moment of collective breath-holding as we all eagerly awaited the start of the performance.

We had enjoyed a pre-concert dinner, and our friend was excited about singing in the chorus. We loved the beautiful sacred music and were preparing for a pleasant evening.

I had been in a relationship with my girlfriend for three years. We socialized with other couples, mostly from her church. She was sensitive and private but disapproved of my being too exuberant.

The four soloists sit on the stage in front of the orchestra during the performance. The men were in tuxedos, and the women were in beautiful gowns. They would stand up for their solos.

With a flourish, the conductor strolled onto the stage and acknowledged the applause with a bow. When he turned to face the orchestra, the auditorium fell into a hushed silence, and we eagerly awaited the first notes of the performance.

The orchestra started with a well-known overture, and the audience held its breath when it ended. Next, the tenor rose, and his voice carried the message of prophecy. Quoting Isaiah 40:1-3, he proclaimed the coming of the Messiah with his "Prepare ye the way of the Lord." It is a moment of profound significance, a call to prepare for the divine.

The tenor finished his solo and sat down, and the audience was silent again.

We were all lured by the beauty of the music, the solemnity of the sacred message, and the formality of the presentation. We were happily settling in for the rest of the performance.

Suddenly, like a jackhammer during the silent prayer at church, **MY PHONE RANG**!

It didn't just ring once; it was a loud, obnoxious ringing that wouldn't stop.

I froze. I knew I had turned my silent switch off before the concert started. How could this happen? I grabbed my phone, but the little red silent switch indicated the phone should be silent—but it kept ringing. I didn't know what to do.

The auditorium was silent except for my loud ringing phone. Thankfully, it went off between the solos and not while they were singing. Everyone was looking at me.

My techie girlfriend reached for my phone to silence it but couldn't.

I panicked, grabbed my phone back, jumped over the overweight senior citizen couple to my left, landed in the aisle, and sprinted to the exit as best as possible in my late 60s.

All this time, my phone kept ringing.

Finally, out in the lobby, I confirmed that my silent switch was set correctly. However, an alarm notification, which I had set the previous day, wasn't affected by the phone's silent switch – and the alarm rang anyway. (Try it sometime on your phone. The phone won't ring, but the alarm will go off even if the silent switch is turned off.)

I turned off the alarm, but my heart was pounding, so I sat in the lobby to calm down. I stayed there until the intermission and then circled and re-entered the auditorium from the other side, hoping no one would notice me.

When I returned to my seat, I apologized to the elderly, overweight couple beside me. He smiled and handed me my pocket calendar, which had popped out when I leaped over them.

My friend and his wife, who sang in the chorus, were understanding. My girlfriend was less so.

I was more than embarrassed or mortified. I felt stupid and humiliated. My girlfriend was not quick to forgive me for embarrassing her.

It was a horrible, embarrassing moment.

I still love The Messiah during the holiday season, but I've learned that the red silent switch isn't sufficient, and now I turn my phone off before the performance starts – or leave it in the car.

Chapter 18: In the Sistine Chapel

The Sistine Chapel at the Vatican Cathedral in Rome is one of the world's most beautiful, reverent, and historic rooms. The story of Michelangelo painting the ceiling frescos in the early 1500s is well known – especially the center image of God giving life to Adam. The Chapel is also famous for hosting the Catholic College of Cardinals when they vote for new popes.

We were on a week-long visit to Italy, three days each in Rome and Florence/Tuscany. Our visit to the Vatican Museum, a sprawling complex of art and history, was a highlight of our trip. The journey to the Sistine Chapel, the museum's crown jewel, was through a labyrinth of corridors, passing through multiple display areas and enduring long queues.

Little did I know during our visit that I would do something that, in hindsight, I can only describe as stupid and embarrassing.

We passed through several smaller chapels with historical paintings on the walls and ceilings, and after waiting in line again, we entered the Sistine Chapel. Its artistic grandeur and immensity struck us: It is 134 feet long and 44 feet wide—larger than a basketball court.

It is one of Italy's prime tourist attractions, and this day was no exception, as it was full of visitors staring at the beautiful walls and 68-foot-high painted ceilings.

It is beyond comprehension to imagine Michaelangelo working high on scaffolding to paint those frescos. The phrase artistic genius doesn't do justice.

I was told there were signs saying photographs were prohibited, but they didn't register with me. The scene was so spectacular that I couldn't resist pulling out my cell phone and taking several pictures – my first stupid mistake.

Several Vatican policemen confronted me about the pictures. It wasn't easy to understand that they were official because they were short and wore unusual uniforms. I thought this was a joke.

They asked for my camera, and I made my second stupid mistake by handing it to my friend. Why? I'll never know. He had more common sense and promptly handed it back.

At this point, the official "Gendarme" asked to see the pictures I'd taken of the ceiling (six stories above us) and demanded that I delete them.

I envisioned time in an Italian jail, so I promptly deleted the images and showed my camera to him. He seemed satisfied and walked away.

I read later that they feared photographic flashes would damage the valuable and unreplaceable fresco paintings.

I felt extremely stupid and embarrassed before my girlfriend and travel companions. I apologized profusely, and my friends were gracious and laughed it off.

My girlfriend was mortified and less forgiving. Soon after we returned home, she handed me her keys to my condo, said she was breaking up with me and walked away.

I'm still embarrassed about this incident. My friends have forgiven and forgotten, and I get together with them periodically with my new wife.

About the Author

John Sower lives with his wife outside of Washington, DC. He has always enjoyed the humor and says these stories have been in his mind for years, if not decades and all he needed to do was sit down with a computer, and the stories told themselves.

- This is the third in a series of Humorous Short Stories:
- "Snow Golf" - Humorous Short Stories about Golf
- "Seventy-Year ITCH" - Humorous Short Stories about Senior Dating
- "No Helmet" - Humorous Short Stories about Embarrassing Moments in Sports

All are available on Amazon.

John Sower

www.ingramcontent.com/pod-product-compliance
Lightning Source LLC
Chambersburg PA
CBHW050306120526
44590CB00016B/2518